MW00715816

Celestial Navigation

Celestial Navigation

Poems by Ellen Jane Powers

Cherry Grove Collections

© 2013 by Ellen Jane Powers

Published by Cherry Grove Collections
P.O. Box 541106
Cincinnati, OH 45254-1106

ISBN: 9781625490353
LCCN: 2013944180

Poetry Editor: Kevin Walzer
Business Editor: Lori Jareo

Visit us on the web at www.cherry-grove.com
Author website: www.ellenjanepowers.com

Cover: "Rosa Celeste" by Gustave Doré

ACKNOWLEDGEMENTS

I would like to thank the editors of the following publications in which these poems first appeared, sometimes in slightly different form:

The Comstock Review: "Four Seasons of Moons,"
  "Reflecting the Day"
The Deronda Review: "Psalm of the Storm,"
  "On the Spirit Road," "For the Light of Jerusalem"
Inspirit: "Hildegard von Bingen"
Kerem: "The Transformation of Jacob"
Lynx Eye: "God has moved"
Pudding: "The Salvation of the World Depends on You"
Raving Dove: "Sisters"

For the Beloved

I blossom in your shade
And taste your love.
— Song of Songs

With gratitude to my mentors:
Ottone "Ricky" Riccio, John McCoubrey,
Chase Twichell, Alfred Corn

Table of Contents

I. Action

Feeding the Day.. 13
Unlocking the Sky... 14
The Salvation of the World Depends on You.. .15
Three Blind Mice.. 16
After Rain.. 17
Numerology... 18
Desert Wanderings.. 20
Pathways of Pine... 21
Four Seasons of Moons...................................... 23
The Voices We Hear... 25
Shape Shifting... 28
An Off-air Melisma.. 30

II. Devotion

Progression from Solitude.................................. 33
Song of the Sister... 35
Four Ways to Water a Garden............................ 36
Illumination... 38
Frère Jacques... 39
Between Me and the Garden Way..................... 40
Between You and the Garden Way.................... 41
Reflecting the Day.. 42
Psalm of the Storm... 43
The Transformation of Jacob............................. 44
Leaving Paradise... 45
The Naming... 46
Antiphon for Eve... 47
Antiphon for Miryam... 48
Down in the Well... 49

III. Contemplation

God has moved.. 53
The Telling... 54
Rabbi Akiba's Account of Ascending to the
    Seventh Heaven....................................... 55
Hildegard von Bingen.................................... 58
Disappearing Act... 59
For the Light of Jerusalem.............................. 60
Feast of the Holy Encounter........................... 62
Sisters... 63
On the Spirit Road... 64
Twinkle Twinkle 65
A Week of Arrivals... 66
Three Ways to Join with You........................... 68
Spring Snow.. 70
Three Songs of Lazarus................................... 71
Celestial Navigation....................................... 73

I. Action

Feeding the Day

The sun is keeping me
inside the cool open-air
room—a shadow box
with a vase of spotted hosta
between me and the balcony.
As I lie on the hotel room couch
a yellow-bellied songbird comes in,
lands on the flared glass lip, turns
toward my edge, pauses
in her glance at my fading form
—broken, dulled.
We study each other, then
she returns to sunshine, and I
to the barren, yellowed shade.
I fill a thick glass ashtray
with water, step into the heavy light,
leave it on the railing where
I can watch from my place inside.
She returns, sips the sunlit water—
as if she knew it would be there.
"The songbird came," I tell
him later, "because
she gave me her request—"
He laughs: *you just indulged
your own desire. Do you take
the requests of lizards, spiders, toads?*
Yes, I think. Yes
—I might even hear the stones
if they sang for an evening meal.

Unlocking the Sky

Each year you reminded me of the black
and blue cry of my own birth, the breech
delivery that pulled your pulse toward it.
You told me my wailing was a bitter awakening
to a human form separated from everything,
and you knew from the sound I wouldn't stay easily.

This year on your birthday, when I call and sing to you,
bless you for your presence that's held me here
since birth, and recall to you, mother,
how I cried, how I wept at my own coming,
you had forgotten the story—
the stroke having blocked it from your own body.

But you had told me I cried, mother! How I cried
at my entrance into this world of sharp-eared dogs
that chase and bite small children mailing letters
at the corner postbox. You heard my wound, mother,
not from you, but for the heaviness of walking
on pavements to schools, to playgrounds never having
enough green—never enough green.

Don't you remember, mother, telling me this sorrow,
your tears for the child who didn't want
to arrive to hairbrushes and dull brown coats
and mittens, who wanted to jump instead
into an endless sky, the seat of the swing
twisting from its sudden loss of weight,
swinging, alone, earthward, as I let go.

The Salvation of the World Depends on You

i.

You walk up the slanted, granite steps,
don't even notice the posting of the sermon,
a citation from the Old Holy Book.
The granite is cold with the dusk,
and the black railing, peeling and rusted.
Why don't you stop and hold the door for the stranger?

ii.

Sitting next to you in the front seat of an automobile,
I wonder why the world is so small.
Really, a one-seater universe.

iii.

You walk past the worn, granite steps,
the yellowed bulletin board with the faded quotation,
a passage from someone's old book.
Do you hear coins dropping in the gutter?
Why not look back? Why not read the passage
peeling off the skin of some salty, stained board?

Three Blind Mice

See how they run beneath the draping forsythia,
their reddish brown bodies like leftover oak leaves.

They all ran, after the cardinal and the junco
flew in for thrown seed, for the shelter of the bush.

The farmer's wife, whose auburn hair has grown dull,
dries flowers and cattails for the winter.

She cuts off their tails, saves the smoke-brown caps
for wreaths of eucalyptus or of rose buds.

With a carving knife she removes false stalks,
saves the blooms and symmetrical leaves for a wire frame.

(Has he ever seen the red dusk of evening in her drying shed?)
She lays them out on a layer of gray newsprint with crisp edges,

such a sight in her life similar to ink-black mice found
stiffened in a speckled birdseed barrel. She shuts the door.

After Rain

My odorless autumn breath
mists in the air before me.
I see a yellow birch shudder
with the orbiting wind.
Full light descends to the stream's
surface, crowning exposed rocks.
Looking in, I see a mosaic
of pebbles and sky—but
I am not there.

Numerology

One

Stop words in light. Watch their sweet sounds drop off tongues—
Oxblood and endless, changing for no one soul.
Lowing today. Tomorrow, courage.
Future days offer a lone light, daughter.

Two

This orange house divides to treat the shame.
Your two hands mend its division from
True balance, maleness moved to one side.
Help the whole, join with your mirrored image.

Three

Pressed yellow buttercups, waxed in time,
Preserved as head and torso with stemmed legs,
Wail a triad of yellowed love.
Daughter, be still, do you hear its voice inside?

Four

Night's doors open, sweating mares follow you till
Green winds bring earth smells, and fire and green water
Eat your night away. Within morning's stand, wash
Due north, and give west your open, parted mouth.

Five

Changing windows of night, your slow dreams travel past
Autumn's sugar maples, their light gone to root.
Don't let seeds quell your freedom. In touching your
Hair, can you feel the blue action life gives?

Six

Beyond your words and thoughts, she exists in you—
Her clear balance nailed to indigo harmony.
Watch. Wait. Know the service that gives her
Within you like a flame in free fall.

Seven

This sword guards spirit wisdom with melodies
Not heard—complete and violet, brightening aura of
Sound! Daughter, dance along the marshland, can you
Feel the bells' sounds wash over your coupling bodies?

Eight

Fence power, judgment, pink roses gardening
Your yard. Will sons and brothers kiss your strength,
Whispering, *catch me, catch me*? Open
One center, but leave the wild briar growing.

Nine

Days' wonder briefly living to tell order
Ends here in this, the day of unsounding humanity.
Gold serpents stretch the length of kingdoms
Not on this earth—Daughter, do you live on?

Desert Wanderings

In the wilderness bordering the sea

You didn't have to bring anything
—and you didn't. You have a brass spine
for carrying yourself, and dark hair,
uncurled as every desire you keep.
I've been carrying a multitude of roses,
but there's been no place for them here.
I see now, even your arms couldn't have held them.

In the wilderness between the walls

A whole but empty eggshell,
its potential blown out,
looks like any carton-kept egg—
until you lift it you won't know
there's a difference—
but you never have.

In the wilderness of lurking places

As if your conclusion—*you are not me*—
could change me into an unclouded mirror.
But its reflection would still resonate with
what I have long desired—
Where are you? *Where are you?*

Pathways of Pine

i.

The pine grove stalks the edge of the field
ripe with mullein and sweet goldenrod.
The sharp narrow needles pierce the sunlight,
stop it from seeping in.

ii.

There's no numbness, just an emptiness when
I look in and see you're not there completely,
that I'm not there at one with you.
It's a pining that will have my life.

iii.

Twenty souls stand between you and me and
that doesn't count the red pine languishing outside my front door.

iv.

Honey, figs, purple, and balm lie out on the cedar table.
Is this not abundance?

v.

Apply turpentine here on your skin. It will stop
the irritation from spreading.

vi.

Next to the fireplace, a brown woven basket
full of grayed pine cones. I throw a brittle cone into the fire,
hear the wail of someone consumed.

vii.

The cellist slowly rosins the filaments of her bow
with the D still resonating.

viii.

The ground pine, bloomed a soft-yellow and spread
over the earth on which I walk, anoints my bare feet.
Its resinous odor sticks to my sandals for weeks
before I realize this is not new.

Four Seasons of Moons

Winter

A cold moon rises in the reddening of twilight.
She stands by the window,
spooning light covers her face,
her shadow-spirit draws near the pairing wolves
breaking snow-covered ground.
She hears their joined howls, and the north wind,
entering through the seams of her door.
Taking a dried leaf of anise, she places it
under her tongue. And swallows.

Spring

Stenciled pines brush the pale morning sky.
The worm moon fades from view.
From the stale, crusted snow, she uncovers
the creeping twinflower and crocus, pink, full-flowered.
The nine herbs of the world are planted in her garden,
its soft earth leaves broken passages of wolves.

Summer

Mountain laurel spills red in the undergrowth,
rising erect and green at the edge of the wood.
The strawberry moon never turns in its ascent, and
she watches as no light penetrates its surface.
Distant thunder vibrates along the surface of her skin,
pauses. Her indigo shawl drops from her shoulders,
she wraps it tight across her breasts.

Autumn

Copper birches flail in the air of the evening turning.
Rose honeysuckle and yellow pears infuse
her garden with an unruly scent, the harvest moon
expands in the east. The beaver hunts greens for its nest,
quailing before no one, not even she, who rests
on the bank, reflecting the water's rippling edge.

The Voices We Hear

Your life shall hang in doubt before you.
—Deuteronomy 28:66

Blessing

This is a blessing—kiwis, blood oranges, mangos
in the northeast. It's still white,
snows layering the ground, and it smells
unlike the humid crop of bananas and papayas
waiting for the blade of gathering.
This is a blessing—to open the door
to sidewalks and traffic lights. Keyholes
with dark centers and large window panes
separate and divide the space,
the coming in and going out.

Chorus of the Angels of Rigorous Ministry

Down we go, to the left of eternity,
to rise with machine-kneaded bread,
the changing of borders. Down we go,
refusing to speak out. We catch you
disregarding the widow, your need
for an excess, your belated care of the parent.
Down we go, to the left of judgment.

Doom

It's daughters, available shall we say,
to fathers for the pleasure of being
conceived. And children, kicked and slapped,
beacons of tranquility, absorb
their insecurities, their burning desires—flames
shoot up past the roof, yet
without notice.

Chorus of the Angels of Merciful Ministry

Here we are, here, in each moment,
each moment someone surges with an impulse
of human connection and completes the thought—
the action expands with such a force,
we drive it down, anxious
for the moment to ignite—the kind stranger,
the anonymous donor, the thief
who cannot kill—

Blessing

This is a blessing—having meat and cheese,
wool and down, handled with the knowing.
This is a blessing—having pillows cradle
our dreams each night and dust-gray branches
of McIntosh turn green in spring rains.

Doom

Why did you turn away, let the door go?—
When did you forget the connection,
the dependence on the farm laborer, the school
bus driver, the bystander? Why did you turn away—
expecting pennies from the jar?

Chorus of Grace

Whoever thought we'd be kept
so small. The world's not what it seems—
if only you saw the threads of light

grounding the illusion. The real kingdom,
not up there, nor to the left or the right,
moves with the moment—found
between the wall outside and
what's held in.

Shape Shifting

I'm slowly awakening
from this dream—
a woman,
in a burning house,
sits with a cup
of peppermint tea,
sees flaming rainbows
edge out
the walls around her.
She doesn't know she's living
within fire—
its warm,
velvety light hums softly
compared to the pitch and roll
of her nightmares.
I'm now at the crosspoint of dreams—
a moment of blinded
stillness,
the body recounting its cells.
I know
there's a fire—
its greenish-blue consummation
scales my skin with
its vapor.
Looking
at my hand,

the dream-shift stops,
and all my vision's
a smeared red sky
turning over
in the closing dark.

An Off-air Melisma

Sor-
   I feel myself slip on the night—
rows
   someone to catch me, not sought,
of
   the fall, a means to join my deboned self—
death
   the cadent darkness coaxes me, and I come—
com-
   sleep intrudes, encases my body,
passed
   which is not ready for the marriage
me
   to the one my soul thrusts toward.

II. Devotion

Progression from Solitude

1.

Gray, early spring rains uncover
crocus uncurling beneath the snow—
but you, you come armed
with desire, protected
by the noon's light taking in your shadow.
I see you reach for me—
your folded stance erected
by the low tremor of my song.
Where is the shivering rain to expose you
fully to the crescendo rising within me?

2.

The polar language of your eyes
turns the corner of my vision—
your exhale taken by my inbreath,
in between, the death-point shared.
Our eyes exchange one word across
the white-noised distance: — now.

3.

If I were dressed in flowers,
they wouldn't be thin red roses.
I'd wear yellowing toadflax,
rays of violet asters, and foxglove,
shady blue. I'd enter the room
where you sit by the fire
reading the world in twilight.
Looking up, you'd see neither me

nor the flowers——our combined scent
opening your vision to the dark
starburst looming within me.

Song of the Sister

Wondering about her darkened lover, she stirs by the window.
He calls like a rock dove to her, a prisoner by the window.

The flower shepherd leaves his shadow on the hillside.
The night whistles like a messenger by the window.

Hear the city cry out against her almond-dark desire.
Her refuge is a moon-drenched comforter by the window.

Wildflowers scent the eastern wind as he wanders.
She steeps herself in an air of lavender by the window.

He cannot find her in the noisy light of midnight.
Alone, she cries in her cedar bed, unheard, by the window.

Nearby, he tends mountain-stained fields with longing,
And she hears his seeds open to flowers by her window.

Four Ways to Water a Garden

1.

She gets a bucket—
the old, dented, gray one
her father once used—
walks to the community well.
The path, a ledge along the meadow
mosaicked with crimson and gray-headed coneflowers,
and vanilla grass, bronzing the morning air.
She inhales. A vision of sky on earth—
her only thought.

2.

A low sky, thunder-blue, wraps
around her as she fills her bucket
from the aqueduct on her father's land.
The sky makes no sound when she lifts
the pail, full of tomorrow's rain.
No crows fly overhead.

3.

After a blacking night, full of dream-colors,
the horizon slides down over the sun.
She wakes to a different sky, helps
her father turn on the long-pipe irrigator,
cuts snapdragons and tiger lilies one by one
in the light dreams make.

4.

The earth's quiet turning reaches
the light so rhythmically she forgets
the passing darkness keeps her
alive. It rains deep enough
for roots to overrun. She notices
a lone tulip, apple-red, near the edge
of her father's garden, never watered
but by a passing rain.

Illumination

I'm afraid of the sunlight
disturbing my eyes with temptation—
I've closed the blinds against
this illusive spectrum. Still,
it finds me through the ill-fit shade
—what it wants
is nothing short of continuance.
I reject its particles, refuse
the host of its resurrection. I want
a dark, dreaming sky, moonless,
to solemnize my need for shadow,
to take from my language
any preservation of self.

Frère Jacques

Are you sleeping on the garden bench shaded in purple
Like David's psalms of praise orienting sunlight?

Brother John told the western wind his pagan name
Before rains lapped the parchment of his amen.

Morning bells are ringing in the abandoned abbey,
Its unanswered prayers cloaking the blue rosemary.

Din, dan, don sound the shadows of your waking,
Catching your lips on those first unsayable words.

Between Me and the Garden Way

I'm becoming as she was: —
unspoken words sacrificed
on the altar of my inner temple.
My heart cannot burn them,
cannot cauterize its own piercing, these
turtledove offerings, swallowed.

He edges serpentine-spotted stone
along a row of purple-stalked hosta.
There is no spirit road here—he is
building it, muscling the earth into place:—
granite, sandstone, fire rock.

Her own unspent words had torn open
the sack of her heart. I have reflected
on her untended form—a leak fills her:
her eyes darkened into refractive pools.

Yellow clusters from the linden dampen
the dirt where he dug in sea holly and
sweet pea by the emerging path.

I want him to plant a white birch to filter
the vermilion moonlight of early fall,

that I may strap my heart, then, with its red-soaked leaves.

Between You and the Garden Way

If I were a ghost wandering your landscape,
My heart transparent in the trapped air you breathe,

You'd walk right through me in your garden
As I came to smell autumn rain on the apples:

You walk unshaken through the wind I've become.
And I, unmoving, feel the weight of your earthen body.

I let you pass through untouched—my desire for you
Burns like lightning though I am barely breath.

Under the sun-turned leaves of your lone fruit tree,
I watch you spend limp flowers from the dahlias.

The soil, the casual rains and sun, and your labored breathing
May not cultivate even one blossom, yet, each spring

You start again, summer's colors illuminated
As you dig through your unspent prayers.

Reflecting the Day
for Aunt Hanna

Aunt is distracted by nuthatches shuttling
birch bark and grass clippings to the birdhouse.
When did I lose her? During talk of living wills and
organ donations, her husband dead these last two years,

or of her living, her finances, accounts in two countries,
names and arrangements known only to herself.
One nuthatch moves headfirst down the tall white pine,
brushes its beak across the trunk, back and forth,

back and forth, proclaiming tree and wooden box
its nesting home. The other brings a scraggy twig,
turns upright, bobs into the hole, its sides chewed
and gnawed from last year's squirrel invasion.

"It's fascinating," she finally says, "this entertainment
right in your backyard." Is it entertaining?
I'm thinking of healthcare and quality of life,
of wordless desires for living out the days,

of shadow-selves revealed in long winter nights.
She spends the afternoon watching the pair, surveys
the feeders now and then for goldfinches and cardinals.
Yesterday a bird slammed into the large pane of glass

and broke its neck, a small tawny sparrow. "Only
a sparrow," Aunt said. Yes, just a common sparrow
who tried to fly through the house to the reflecting trees
                              and brightening sky beyond.

Psalm of the Storm

I hear the east wind
      blow across the heavens,
      the sycamores cradle the frost.

We were like them, in that dream,
      in the day of fig-filled branches
      empty of green leaves.

Do you remember: the quail sang
      for her mate, and the east wind
      answered with another's call.

What signs does the desert give
      under star-lined skies, and what signs
      do mountains take from rock-faced nights?

I call to you, to remember
      the dreaming, when the hard frost
      tore my skin and only your fruit remained.

The Transformation of Jacob

There's only one way out of the ravine
as night curls into the ridge of balsam—
and that is, to leave your name behind.

Shadows fall over your hairless arm,
and this night the gate to heaven opens
as dark curls into the ridge of balsam.

When the earth twin's hands crown you, the wind
is your struggle—you balance its weight against you
because this night the gate of heaven is open.

When it pushes the smooth hollow of your thigh,
you ask for its blessing, unwilling to let it go
from your struggle, balancing its strength against you.

"Bless me, unnamed one." You hold its hairy arms—
the predawn light angles over the rocky cliffs—
you ask again for its blessing, unwilling to let it go.

You, O Go-straight-to-God, you no longer hold my heel!
There's only one way out of the ravine
in the predawn light angling over the rocky cliffs—
and that is, to leave your old name behind.

Leaving Paradise

I dreamt you split in two.
One of you left to reenter
that other world
where tulips flag in another's hands.
The other stayed
and turned to face me,
unsure what part remained.
He joined the wheel of his heart
to my own. I woke
failing to see who you are,
craning to see who we've become.

The Naming

Everything Adam named died. And
we continue that pronouncement—every
newborn Adam and Eve is called to death.

If I forget my name, what?—
You remember it. Say it. Each of its vowels
vibrates in your throat, reverberates
in the labyrinth of my own ear.

But I remember it differently—
I fell out of the sky into my mother's womb,
my other name lost inside her flesh.

Each autumn I breathe the biting scent of decay
and feel the turning of my name—
to the name that makes me feel a stranger,
to the one she couldn't recompose
though it had throbbed deep within her.

Antiphon for Eve

You walked among green fig trees
On the sixth day, certain your other side
Joined you with the same cloudless breath.
After separating, when did the Light,
Striking with shadowy presence,
Show you the flaming tree whose taste
Burned down the gate? Having become flesh,
Become mother, where is the place
The daughter of One now dwells, your skin
Thickened, your mouth dry from earth's words?

Do you still tremble when caught in a stormy wind,
Still remember as she moves among us unheard?

Antiphon for Miryam

In the wilderness she dampened
Their grief with thumps on her timbrel,
Pulled away their wailing desire
For fields of scarlet bittersweet.

Fragrant rock-waters near wormwood and indigo
Suffused the Egypt within her.
The thunderless fountain, her holy death-spot,
Now weeps with an aroma of myrrh.

Hear her cry when a faceless moon
Shadows the cedars and opens the skies.
Hear her cry in the thunder of dreams
When she urges the dark to sing in reply.

Down in the Well

God's in my basement.
I smelled its anguish seeping
through the fieldstone foundation
like the smell of earth
clawed by a summer thunderstorm.

God's in my basement!
Trickled in somehow between
the heart beam and stone, and
reassembled as a damp spirit
weeping beneath my life.

I smell its presence rising
through the floorboards
each time I burn with sorrow,
my skin tingling like pages wrinkling
from the dampness of neglect.

III. Contemplation

God has moved

and left no forwarding address
and he took st. nicholas too
they're riding some stellar sleigh
easing through the universe
admiring stars beyond the milky way
laughing and joking
about planting a new eden
far away from here
no seeds of adam in this new garden
no, the children of adam must stay behind
must stay in this now godless galaxy
hopefully someone will have the good sense
to send a space probe an e-mail of sorts
to seek-out god asking him to return
asking him at the very least
to send back st. nicholas

The Telling

I am dark, daughters of Jerusalem, and I am beautiful!
—Song of Songs 1:5

Tell me, sister, how safflower stains your lips
a deep red, how turmeric blends your nails
with a hue the shade of the morning sun.

Tell me how the half-moon affects your rhythm,
how starless nights quicken your sunbathed skin,
how water, blue with the night, restores you.

Tell me, sister, how your body knows the fields,
knows the yellow tansy and purple clover,
knows the blades of flourishing grass —

Tell me, for the other comes to mow my field this night,
and I must be the keeper of my own garden.

Rabbi Akiba's Account of Ascending to the Seventh Heaven

1. Going Down in the Chariot

How prepared am I to journey to the Throne,
To journey to Heaven while I still live on earth.

As for those before me?—the first one died,
The second, now a madman, and the third,

The third has turned his back on my Lord.
I bind my forearm, taste the Teaching

As it presses on my forehead, adheres to my flesh.
I wear the lamb's wool *tallit* of my father,

And the weight of my fathers before me pulls me down,
Deep into the dark absence of my self.

2. In the Halls of Heaven

I contemplate the Name, the upper worlds, their flowing
Streams of thought. A snowy veil parts, revealing

A craggy bridge across a starless chamber. I walk
Among fiery spheres coming and going. One of them

Pitches toward me—the Name, still guarding my lips,
The faint horizon, my destination—I do not stop.

I know this place. The signs of Heaven are unveiled
To the prophets in the hall where I now stand.

Gabriel permits few to enter, and I must not tremble.
The light of *Shekinah* knells within me, and I am hers.

My eyes start to sting as the rumbling sky opens—
Millstones of the Universe are evenly turning,

Grinding out Time behind me. What light there is
Is darker than when I first crossed over, and I sing the Name,

All the Names in thanksgiving. In lightless light
The Heavenly Temple of Jerusalem intersects these worlds.

Mikhael opens the Gate before me, spilling its silence.
I remember—the desire to stay is overwhelming.

Holy, holy, holy is the Divine, I sing it aloud,
And it echoes all around me, its bass falls heavily from

The beam on which I stand. Holy, holy, holy ripples along
The shell-like ceiling, turning the color of camphor with each note.

The whole earth is filled with Yah's glory! The ripening hum
Of an unseen chorus bleeds my ears, and I stand erect

With my mouth stammering the praises within me.
I am penetrated by the cutting chords of the Endless.

3. *The Presence*

The mountainous iron doors of the final chamber open.
A creature of fire carrying a scroll stands before me.

Metatron, Servant of the Divine, setting his gaze upon me,
Steps aside to reveal the Throne of the Presence—

I feel my knees tremble with my own inner pulse,
Feel my life-source pulse the joy and fear of oneness,

Feel the translucence beneath me—the flames around me
Begin their consummation, and I hesitate—

4. *Descent to Earth*

Shaking, I feel a wind brush across my face. Turning,
I see the Great Hall as dense smoke in the distance.

I am aware of my presence. I hurry to the gates
Behind me, keeping the Name on my tongue,

Watching the stones below me jag and pitch with an
Emptiness I feel along the bottoms of my feet.

No one takes notice as I soberly move through
The lower halls to the seat of my own body,

Which has waited for me, bound to my fathers before me,
To the earth on which I sojourn. I, Rabbi Akiba,

Have been to Heaven and lived to tell about it, knowing
I must keep these words in the book of my soul

And burn any record—for each letter, each syllable,
Must be returned as I was returned to this world as one.

Hildegard von Bingen

I was a tithe—
from my parents' wealth of children,
given as spirit companion to Jutta
the recluse. My visions from childhood
were never shared but with those I served.
My means have been simple, and the evening
shadow has brought only sweet sleep.
Let it be known I was in no place
of worship when a voice such as could only
be said was from heaven spoke, no,
commanded me to make what is hidden
plain as the pasture rose that grows in the sand.
The voice followed me even as my body
repelled its words and lay within the rib of day.
So I write what I have seen and felt in open spaces,
a lion among a herd of antelope, grasslands aflame,
a fiery breath moving over us—my old skin
melts away and I am again a sweet maid-child.

Disappearing Act

I don't want to love you any more
than I already do. Yet
each day your morning's rise
sinks more deeply within me.
Make this falling stop!
Its weight will force
the air from my lungs, and
I'm afraid
the only breath left to me
will be your own.

For the Light of Jerusalem

Fiery center

Morning glories among dark fields of grain
revel in a morning's amber light
on a postcard you and I view
of the supplicating hills of Jerusalem.

Empty names

A red wind chastens an undivided willow
along the river Jordan like a mournful harp.
Seven times we've crossed over on our way south,
descending through the garden of God.
You and I remain in that process of being,
for we are that, too, even in Jerusalem.

Silencing silence

Tulips pushing through the late Jerusalem snow
spring upward into bud, breaking light into color.
You and I gather up their ruinous pieces,
place them in the shade of the Lion's Gate
for the slow decay beside the roaring walls
of the northern side of Jerusalem.

Divided from One

The weight of the morning's prayers
lightens the uncapped day, and
the unlit passage of evening, called
by another name, flags like the undersides
of white anemones in a wave of stormy light
moving across the seven hills of Jerusalem.
Under a languishing midnight sky,

you and I enter the city of psalms.

Unmovable darkness upon bare fingers
In the valley of Mount Anointment a scent
of thicket roses charges the night's summer air
and spreads over us, as if we, too, are garden
come into bloom along the walls of Jerusalem.

A space in the heart
The filtered light cannot unfurl the frostweed,
flowerless on this cloudy day, nor turn over
the blue vetch blooming upside down
to face the scorched earth of late summer.
You and I continue our search for wildflowers
along the cobbled streets of Jerusalem,
shadowed now by all our names.

Breath of exile
As we approach, the rock beneath the dome
exhales creation's alphabet, and you and I
breathe in its words like strangers.
We had seen the morning's freeze render pink flax
growing in a thicket as stars on a clear January night,
and now, our words, as many tongued verses
of praise that cleave to the skies of Jerusalem.

Feast of the Holy Encounter

As she lies in a field of blue lupine and pale blue pansies,
she is suddenly overshadowed by his form.
In the halo shattering the sky's light
into a thorny blaze flaring all around him,
she hears the ringing echo of a goldfinch
roll over her like the flight of the bird
and sink her further into the wildflowers.

> *If my heart were weighed, would it be*
> *light enough to admit me into paradise?*

All she can see are thorns of flame
and his form at their dark seraphic center,
so she surrenders her body still further
into the leafy hands of the flowers.

> *Have the sun and I disappeared*
> *with the emergence of your incandescent self?*

She feels the fire he's become warm her flesh, and
her own center detach from the earth's spin
and rise toward him. When he withdraws,
the wind brings a scent of fresh grass,
and day returns to where he was.

Sisters

You were always playing the mother,
ordering me to fetch water, to tear rags
for the wounds our dolls pretended to have.

I saw the shells explode in our village,
the blood, splotched and speckled across the road,
the doorway where we play dolls, stained red.

Your doll shouts, *Flee*! They pack their belongings,
move out onto the street. Which way do we go?
Away! Away from the noise, we answer.

It's quiet. I hear you breathing next to me.
I curl into your back, whispering,
Do you know all girls have the same mother?
You must have heard me. Your breath stopped abruptly.
Gurgling, you said my name. It must be true.

After they took you to hospital, mother died.
Aunt tells me you're in America,
in a place that will give you new legs.

I am waiting for you in the doorway of our house.
I took the legs off your doll, wrapped her with rags,
told her she's not allowed to play outside anymore.

On the Spirit Road

Following a winding path, switch-backed,
limbed with Lebanon and Deodar Cedars,
their branches lifting and drooping,
I breathe the betweenness of this place.
Above me, in unmoving daylight, blue sky,
filled with cerulean and white dots as though
waves of light were caught in strobe.
In the distance, an archway of lilac gray stone,
HaShem, the Name, chiseled into its keystone.
Beyond, blurred like a rainy meadow full of wildflowers.
The road, the cedars, the light, spill
into this winding, winding road, where,
with each step, I, too, pour out looking for you
as the fireweed and steeplebush sway in the rain.

Twinkle Twinkle

Twinkle, twinkle, moonlit fields of sustenance,
the living house opening to stars.

Little stars, distant, their light pulled toward evening,
give sight to those wanderers choiring like snow.

How I wonder, ashes falling from abandoned stars,
at a cloudless night weighing against your skin.

What you are to become empties before me,
and I gather its stones still burning like stars.

Up above the world, a multitude of keyholes,
on the earth, a word for unlocking light.

So high, evening unturns day spooled from stars,
and your season falls past the last days of words.

Like a diamond unearthed from a barren mine,
your radiance sustains the unsleeping house.

In the sky's empty places, I wonder how the dark
bends toward what you will have become.

A Week of Arrivals

Sunday

God named only four things: heaven,
dryland, seas, and the light of day.
In this place where I am, sun-drenched dark
covers your face. Even the divine cannot
remove your sadness willfully. I have only fallen
words for you—armfuls of white lotus petals.

Monday

Of the 248 parts of your soul, I don't know
which one's edge I see in your eyes.
When you look at me, you silently count
my parts as if their sum might startle you.
I wear imperfectly stitched moonlit gauze
to protect me from the silence dividing us.

Tuesday

Finger to finger, palm on palm, our hands touch.
We lift them toward the warring sky.
The trees harbor that blaze within their fruits, and
we stand in a field cooled by lavender and hyssop.
I feel the latched gate to heaven in your hands.

Wednesday

In the fourth day's spirit-bound womb,
male and female embrace as twins. When my lips
touch and part yours, we are at that beginning
before sun and moon argued to be the greatest,
before flowers ceased their blooming.

Thursday

You are the thunder harmonizing
with my inner pulse—my tide held at its turning.
My ivory skin becomes your lightning.
I just now realize who you are.

Friday

In the center of this unworldly land,
crowned with quince and walnut, you plant
a marble fountain to catch parts of heaven
in each drop of rain. The garden is nearly complete,
and my breath will have nowhere to go but out.

Saturday

Lying in a violet flamed bed of lilies,
we are joined by an aural thread. I dream
of a place you are shadow. When I touch your feet,
your name comes to rest in my arms—
white lotus buds opening and opening.
To begin this week, let us make
for each other a new name, one formed
from God's list of dayless words.

Three Ways to Join with You

1. Contemplation

They escaped the garden,
the yellow iris lighting the streamside
by my house—they harbor
the *in-being* of my thoughts.
I walk among their abandonment
and encounter your own thought
in the collapsing sun.
I am aroused by a moment
of balance—
you, on the wild hillside,
facing south to absorb
the last of the full day's light,
and I, taking in a sliver of rainbow,
the yellow-gold bodies of iris,
surrender to the oncoming dark.

2. Devotion

The undersong of this copper evening
flowers the snowdrops hidden in the ivy
beneath my apple tree—
the unifying darkness cannot
separate me from your affection.
I consecrate the white petals
the tree weeps each spring—
my words burn on my tongue,
the purification of a communion wafer
in threefold sanctification of God.
Now, a shower of fragrance covers the ground,
and each morning of the lasting days

I walk barefoot among the flecks, the white spaces
between the letters of my prayer.

3. Action

My body depends on this tree—
a yellow birch scarred by lightning,
infusing the air with the odor of wintergreen.
You know the alliance between us—
the tree, impelled out of this world
despite its affliction, and I,
willful and will-less, commune
with the dark receding soil of my garden.
You inspirit me with your own life's sap.
You want me to act even as the crippled tree—
to reach heavenward and drive the climbing black sky
beyond each day's horizon.

Spring Snow

the time of tight lilac buds
a spring snow   heavy and fresh
covers the surface of things
with a stifling whiteness displacing
greening-browns and red tipped maple branches
this is not a winter palace   this snow-recovered land
crested branches bend down over drives
and red pines slump with the cold weight
crocus and daffodil leafstalks pushed through the thaw
and the early iris   a garden of deep-blue-sky by the wooden fence
are cradled and stacked by this delivery
sun   north-side-earth tilted in its favor   stirs the dense air
moves the snowfall into black pools   yet
at this moment a spring snow covers all these things
and it is so white

Three Songs of Lazarus

1. Song of Remembering

I heard this weeping
during my sleep and
a loud voice like thunder.
My dream parted like a storm,
a sudden wind bending
the branches of a birch,
rattling and shaking its leaves,
twisting the sunlight so it fell
far from its trunk. It is this light
that rolled over my face,
and I woke.

2. Song of Realization

For you I came back
from the curling dark,
from the cold which burned
away my careless tongue.
For you I came back,
flush from wild waters
that left my flesh like a newborn's.
For you I came back,
without the hunger for my life.

3. Song of Resurrection

Blackberries stain my fingers
while I fill my basket with fruits.
In the evening, swallows anguish

under the layering dark, hungry
for their fill. I thought I knew this land,
its bleating sheep and stony hills, yet
everything mourns now without weeping,
and—this new wine and meat, they taste
as if seasoned with sunlight,
as if I were tasting the sky.

Celestial Navigation

What survives the beloved, she asks
during the dark-eyed day of the moon.

Within a walled garden, full of unseen roses,
she walks among their psalms, staking them
against the harsh winds of winter.

What survives the beloved, she asks
under a sliver of the moon's waxing light.

As she walks through her sanctuary,
the stillness that surrounds her
is budding with psalms.

Will I survive the beloved, she asks
in the unconsuming light of a full moon.

The shelter of the garden lies in a shadow
of hemlock as she tends the roses, listening
to the silence of their blooming.

Ellen Jane Powers has had poems and book reviews appear in such journals as *Inspirit, Off the Coast, The Deronda Review, Kerem,* and other journals, and in the anthology *Do Not Give Me Things Unbroken.* A graduate of the Creative Writing Program at Goddard College in Vermont, her first poetry collection, *Celestial Navigation* (Cherry Grove) and chapbook, *Toward the Beloved* (Finishing Lines Press), came out in 2013. She lives in the Boston area.

CPSIA information can be obtained at www.ICGtesting.com
Printed in the USA
BVOW07s1233220713

326506BV00001B/4/P